ADAPTED FOR SUCCESS

SNAKES
AND OTHER REPTILES

Andrew Solway

Heinemann Library
Chicago, Illinois

Photo research by Mica Brancic and Susi Paz
Designed by Richard Parker
Printed and bound in China by WKT Company Ltd

11 10 09 08 07
10 9 8 7 6 5 4 3 2 1

Library of Congress Cataloging-in-Publication Data
Solway, Andrew.
  Snakes and other reptiles / Andrew Solway.
      p. cm. -- (Adapted for success)
  Includes bibliographical references and index.
  ISBN-13: 978-1-4034-8224-2 (library binding (hardcover))
  ISBN-10: 1-4034-8224-1
  ISBN-13: 978-1-4034-8231-0 (pbk.)
  ISBN-10: 1-4034-8231-4
  1. Snakes--Juvenile literature. 2. Reptiles--Juvenile literature. I. Title. II. Series: Solway, Andrew. Adapted for success.
  QL666.O6S676 2006
  597.96--dc22
                                    2006014293

Acknowledgments
The author and publisher are grateful to the following for permission to reproduce copyright material:
Alamy p. 22 (David Hosking); Corbis pp. 31 (Australian Picture Library/Leo Meier), 24 (Chris Hellier), 12 (Frank Lane Picture Agency), 25 (Frank Lane Picture Agency/Ron Austing), 6 (Frans Lanting), 33 (Gallo Images/Rod Patterson), 10 (Gavriel Jecan), 27 (George McCarthy), 23 (Jim Zuckerman), 13 (Joe McDonald), 38 (Kelly-Mooney Photography), 39 (Ludovic Maisant), 37 (Martin Harvey), 9 (Steve Kaufman), 19 (Zefa/Kevin Schafer); Getty pp. 20 (Altrendo), 41 (Lonely Planet Images), 14, 21, 34, 35 (National Geographic), 5, 18 (Stone), 4, 26 (Taxi), 16 (The Image Bank); NHPA pp. 30 (Anthony Bannister), 8, 15, 29 (Daniel Heuclin), 40 (Joe Blossom); Science Photo Library pp. 32 (Alan Sirulnikoff), 43 (Bonnier Publications/Claus Lunau), 28 (William Ervin);
Tim Graham Photo Library p. 36.

Cover photograph of an arboreal snake sensing with its tongue reproduced with permission of Getty Images (National Geographic/Tim Laman).

The publishers would like to thank Ann Fullick for her assistance in the preparation of this book.

Contents

Some words are shown in bold, **like this**. You can find out what they mean by looking in the glossary.

Introduction to Adaptation

An **adaptation** is a change that helps a living thing survive in its **habitat**. What adaptations make a really successful **predator**? How about a small head, poor eyesight and hearing, or a skinny body and no legs? It does not sound like a successful formula. Yet these are the adaptations of snakes, one of the most successful groups of **vertebrate** predators.

Fangs are the main weapon of many snakes. The fangs of a viper or rattlesnake, such as this pygmy rattlesnake, lie against the roof of the mouth until they are needed.

Reptiles rule!

There are about 2,700 known **species** of snake. Snakes are reptiles—a group that also includes lizards, crocodiles, and turtles. There are about 7,700 reptile species in total.

(Turtles are sometimes called tortoises if they live on land. Throughout this book, the word *turtles* is used for the group that includes both tortoises and turtles.)

WHAT IS A REPTILE?

Reptiles are vertebrates such as crocodiles, lizards, turtles, and snakes. Other vertebrates include mammals, birds, **amphibians**, and fish. Unlike other vertebrates, reptiles have dry, scaly skin. Most reptiles lay eggs with shells, although a few species give birth to live young. Reptiles are **cold-blooded** like amphibians and fish.

From roughly 280 million years ago until 65 million years ago, reptiles were the dominant animals on Earth. **Ichthyosaurs** and **plesiosaurs** swam in the sea, while **pterosaurs** soared through the sky. From about 230 million years ago, dinosaurs were the dominant animals on land. Then, about 65 million years ago, something happened that led to dinosaurs and many other reptiles becoming **extinct**.

Snakes spread

In the history of reptiles, snakes are relatively new animals. The oldest snake fossils are from only about 120 million years ago. The first snakes were lizards that became legless as an adaptation to a burrowing lifestyle. Today, most snakes live above ground. There are snakes all over the world, except Antarctica. They live on mountains, in forests, in deserts, and in rivers and seas. There are even a few snakes that can glide through the air. All snakes have adapted in different ways to their habitats.

The head of this iguana shows the dry scaly skin that covers all reptiles.

Secrets of success

What does it mean to say that snakes are successful? How do you measure their success? Several features of snakes have made them successful. Although they have no legs, their long, thin, flexible bodies help snakes glide along the ground quickly. They also can climb, swim, and burrow. Their long, thin bodies are hard to spot, which is good both for sneaking up on **prey** and for hiding from enemies. Even though a snake is very thin, its extremely flexible jaw and stretchy stomach allow it to eat large prey. Many snakes have a **venomous** bite that can paralyze or kill their prey. Snakes that are not venomous kill their prey by squeezing it to death.

How Does Adaptation Work?

Evolution is the process by which life on Earth has developed and changed. Life first appeared on Earth 3.5 billion years ago. Since then, living things have evolved from simple single **cells** to the estimated 10 million or more different species on Earth today.

Male chameleons fight each other for the chance to mate with female chameleons. The best-adapted male will win the fight and mate with the female.

Useful changes

Adaptation is an important part of evolution. Adaptations are ways in which a living thing changes to fit into a particular environment and way of life. For instance, a crocodile's powerful, flattened tail is an adaptation for swimming. A snake's long, thin body was originally an adaptation for burrowing. How, then, does adaptation happen?

Variation

Not all individuals of the same species are exactly the same. You can see this yourself if you look around your class at school. Some people are taller than others. Some people have light hair, while others have dark hair. Some people are musical, some are good at math, and some are good at sports. These differences between individuals of a species are known as **variations**.

ALL IN THE GENES

Living things pass on characteristics to their **offspring** through their **genes**. A living thing's genetic material is a kind of instruction book for that individual.

Most animals and plants produce offspring by sexual reproduction. Males and females each produce special cells, known as **gametes**, which have only half the normal genetic material. Each parent provides half the genetic information for the offspring.

Natural selection

The variation between individuals is what makes it possible for a species to change and adapt. The driving force for adaptation is called **natural selection**. Different species **compete** with each other for space and for food. Individuals of the same species also compete with each other for the best **mates**. The animals that are best adapted to their environment survive to **reproduce** and pass on their useful characteristics.

If there are changes in the environment where a species lives, natural selection will favor those individuals that have some slight difference that gives them an advantage in the new situation. For example, when the ancestors of snakes first began burrowing, natural selection perhaps favored thin individuals with shorter legs because they could move faster underground. Over many generations, thinner animals with short legs were selected, until eventually their bodies became snake-like and their legs were lost altogether.

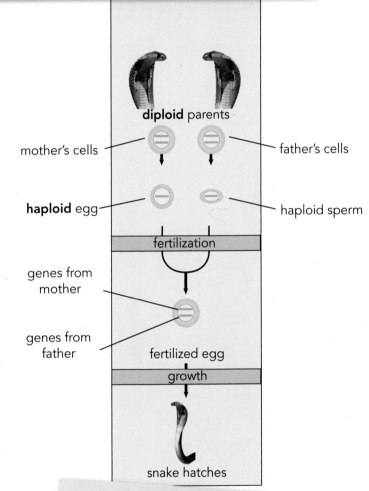

diploid parents

mother's cells — father's cells

haploid egg — haploid sperm

fertilization

genes from mother

genes from father

fertilized egg

growth

snake hatches

This diagram shows the process of reptile reproduction. Each parent produces gametes (egg cells and sperm cells) that are haploid—they have only half the normal genetic material. When the gametes combine, they form a **fertilized** egg with a full set of genes.

Snakes in Many Habitats

Snakes are legless because their ancestors were burrowers. Some snakes, such as pipe snakes and blind snakes, still spend most of their time underground. However, most snakes have abandoned burrows and have adapted to living in other habitats.

Sea snakes have adapted to living in water by developing a flattened body.

Forests, seas, and deserts

Many snakes have adapted to forest life. Snakes that live in trees tend to be thinner and smaller than their cousins that live on the ground. Emerald boas, which live in trees, are much smaller than anacondas, which are ground-living. This adaptation enables the emerald boas to move easily through the trees. There are also many snakes that live in freshwater or in the sea. Sea snakes have bodies that are flattened side to side, especially at the tail. This flattened shape helps them swim efficiently.

Snakes also have adapted to life in extreme environments such as deserts. Saving water is the most important thing for survival in the desert, and a snake's scaly skin is very good at keeping in moisture. To avoid the day's heat, desert snakes are most active at night and rest in burrows during the day. Several desert snakes move in an unusual looping movement called sidewinding. This is a very efficient way to move over sand.

GLIDING SNAKES

A few forest snakes have evolved a quicker way to get around than climbing. Their bodies are adapted to glide from tree to tree. The paradise flying snake can glide up to 328 feet (100 meters). The snake sucks in its stomach and spreads its ribs out sideways, which makes the snake wider. Then it curves its underside upward. The whole body is like a long, thin parachute. In the air the snake makes an *S* shape to keep it stable as it glides.

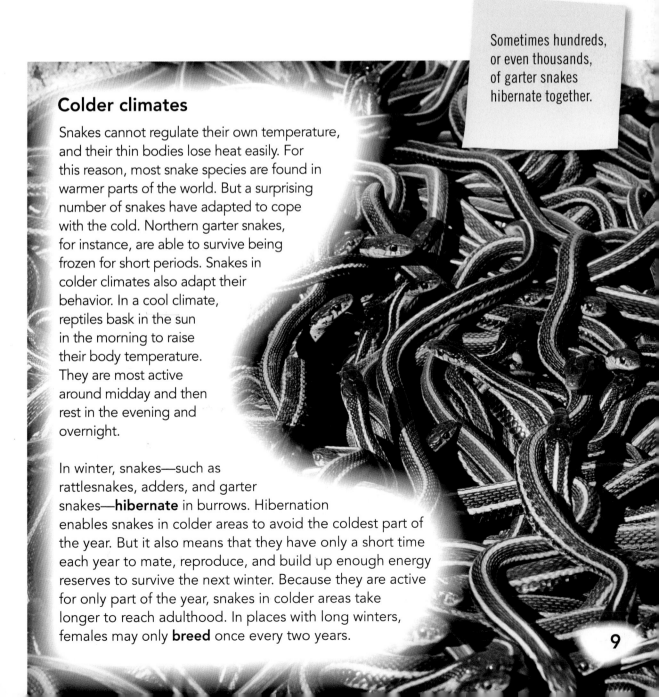

Sometimes hundreds, or even thousands, of garter snakes hibernate together.

Colder climates

Snakes cannot regulate their own temperature, and their thin bodies lose heat easily. For this reason, most snake species are found in warmer parts of the world. But a surprising number of snakes have adapted to cope with the cold. Northern garter snakes, for instance, are able to survive being frozen for short periods. Snakes in colder climates also adapt their behavior. In a cool climate, reptiles bask in the sun in the morning to raise their body temperature. They are most active around midday and then rest in the evening and overnight.

In winter, snakes—such as rattlesnakes, adders, and garter snakes—**hibernate** in burrows. Hibernation enables snakes in colder areas to avoid the coldest part of the year. But it also means that they have only a short time each year to mate, reproduce, and build up enough energy reserves to survive the next winter. Because they are active for only part of the year, snakes in colder areas take longer to reach adulthood. In places with long winters, females may only **breed** once every two years.

Back to the Water

Reptiles were the first of the modern vertebrate groups to adapt fully to life on land. Some amphibians—such as frogs, toads, and their relatives—lived on land before reptiles did, but they needed damp conditions to survive and be active. An amphibian's thin skin loses water quickly, whereas a reptile's scaly skin is waterproof. Amphibian eggs have a jelly-like coating to reduce the risk of drying out, but this is not as effective as the hard or leathery shell of a reptile's eggs.

Although reptiles are well adapted to land life, some species have adapted to life in the water. Crocodiles and alligators spend much of their life in water. Many turtle species also live in water—sea turtles hardly ever touch land their whole lives.

With only their eyes and nostrils showing, crocodiles are almost invisible lurking in the water.

Adapting to water

Crocodiles and alligators (crocodilians) are well adapted to **ambush** prey in the water. A crocodilian's flattened tail is adapted to power it through the water. Its eyes and nostrils are right on top of its head—ideal for lurking just beneath the water's surface with only the eyes and nostrils showing. It can also dive beneath the water and stay there for 15 minutes or longer without breathing.

Crocodilians do not spend all their time in water. They come out on land to sunbathe and warm up their bodies. However, sea turtles do spend their lives in water. Female sea turtles only come ashore to dig a nest and lay their eggs, while male sea turtles never come ashore after leaving their hatching beach. A sea turtle's front and back legs have become flattened into large flippers. The front flippers give most of the swimming power—the turtle flaps its flippers to move through the water. The back flippers trail behind and are used for steering.

DIGGING IN

Some crocodiles have adapted to life in climates that are too cold or too dry by lying **dormant** for part of the year. American alligators dig deep gator holes in the swamp areas where they live to keep themselves cool in warm weather. In winter they dig burrows where they lie dormant through the cold months. Chinese alligators live in large underground burrows in winter. Australian freshwater crocodiles shelter in burrows when rivers dry up in the dry season.

There are seven different species of sea turtle. The largest, the leatherback turtle, can survive the cold at depths of over 3,281 feet (1,000 meters) and in oceans far north and south of the Equator. Leatherbacks can keep their core body temperature as much as 64 °F (18 °C) above the temperature of the water around them. They can do this partly because they have a thick layer of fat beneath their skin, which **insulates** them from the cold. In addition, their blood system is adapted to help them stay warm. Warm blood coming from the core of the body into the flippers warms up cold blood returning from the flippers into the body.

As cold blood comes back from a turtle's flipper, it meets warm blood coming from the body. The blood coming out warms the blood going back to the body, and this helps the turtle stay warm.

warm blood from body

cold blood coming back from flipper

Swimming in Sand, Walking on Water

There are 4,560 species of lizard—more than any other reptile, including snakes. They have adapted to fit into a wide range of different habitats. On land lizards are more widespread and numerous than any other reptile. However, only a few lizards are good swimmers, while the marine **iguana** is the only species found in the ocean.

Sandfish have a very smooth, polished skin that helps them glide through the sand.

Lizards in deserts

Lizards are more at home in deserts than any other animals. Because it is so hot by day, many lizards stay underground where it is cooler. They come out to feed in the evening or at night.

One group of geckos that live in the desert have webbed feet. They do not use their feet for swimming but for scooping sand. Another group of lizards known as sandfish swim through loose sand by wriggling their bodies.

Agile climbers

Many lizard species are adapted to live in forests. These lizards are generally long-legged and agile. They run along branches and jump between trees. Chameleons are good climbers, but they move very slowly. Their claw-like feet can grip branches powerfully, and they can use their tail as a fifth leg, wrapping it around a branch for extra stability.

Geckos are another group of excellent climbers. Their feet have large claws or pads covered with millions of tiny hairs that give them a grip, even on glass. The flying dragons of Southeast Asia probably have the best way of getting around in the forest. They have large flaps of skin on the sides of their bodies, strengthened by elongated ribs, which open out to form wings. Flying dragons can glide about 200 feet (60 meters) between trees.

LEGLESS LIZARDS

Snakes are not the only group of legless reptiles. Other lizards also have become **specialist** burrowers and have lost their legs in the process. Slow worms and snake lizards are just two of several lizard species that look very similar to snakes. Another group of reptiles, the worm-lizards, also look like snakes although they are not snakes, lizards, or worms!

A basilisk lizard is caught in action, running over the water surface.

Walking on water

Although few lizards are regular swimmers, one kind of lizard can walk on water. Basilisk lizards have long toes on their back legs, with flaps of skin along the sides to increase the area of each toe. When it is in danger, the basilisk runs away on its back legs. With its extra-large feet, streams and ponds are no problem—the basilisk just keeps running over the surface of the water.

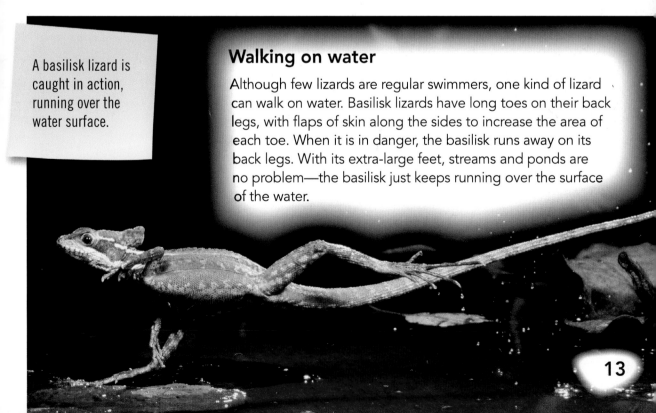

Fanged Hunters

All snakes are predators, but they hunt a wide range of different foods, from insects to mammals as large as deer or even crocodiles. Snakes have many adaptations that help make them successful hunters.

Eyes and ears

Snakes often have poor eyesight and hearing. This is because they lost much of their vision and hearing when they first evolved as burrowing animals. Today, snakes that live on the surface do have eyes, but they are different from those of other animals. Other vertebrates focus by changing the shape of the **lens** in the eye. Snakes, however, focus by moving the lens closer to or farther away from the **retina**. This kind of eye does not work as well as the eyes of other animals.

Snakes have poor hearing for sounds that travel through the air—the sounds that humans hear well. This is because snakes do not have an external ear opening. However, they can hear vibrations through the ground fairly well.

A snake's nose is on the roof of its mouth. It is called the Jacobson's organ.

Super senses

To make up for their poor eyesight and hearing, snakes have an excellent sense of smell. Snakes do have nostrils but, instead, have smell sensors in two small pits in the roof of the mouth. The snake tastes the air with its forked tongue, then puts the ends of the tongue into its smell sensors. The sensors pick up any scents caught on the tips of the tongue.

Some snakes, including pit vipers and most boas and pythons, are very sensitive to heat. They have heat sensors on their face that pick up tiny changes in temperature. This helps them track small mammals and birds by picking up the heat they give off.

No chewing

Snakes have no teeth to chew up their food —they have to swallow it whole. With such a narrow head and body, snakes should be limited to eating small prey. Snakes can open their jaws very wide, however, and the bones of their skull can actually move apart to allow large pieces of food to pass.

Snakes that eat insects, frogs, or other small animals simply swallow them whole and alive. Snakes that attack larger prey need to kill them before they eat them. They use one of two methods. Constrictor snakes wind themselves around their prey and squeeze them until they cannot breathe. Venomous snakes have poison fangs that they sink into their prey. The poison paralyzes or kills the prey.

DIFFERENT BODIES

A snake's body shape is adapted to the way it feeds. Snakes such as the gaboon viper are sit-and-wait hunters. They are heavy and thick-bodied because they do not need to move fast. Instead, they need strength when they strike. Snakes such as whip snakes and black racers are fast movers that chase their prey. These snakes have long, thin bodies for getting over the ground quickly.

This egg-eating snake has dislocated its jaw completely. This allows the snake to open its mouth wide enough to swallow the egg.

Other Ways of Feeding

Reptiles eat many different foods, ranging from underwater plants to buffalos. However, most reptiles are **carnivores**. Crocodiles and alligators are predators of fish and large animals. Many lizards eat insects, although large iguanas eat plants. Most turtles are also predators. However, many turtles eat plants as well as animals, and some species are **herbivores**.

Crocodiles and alligators

Crocodiles and alligators are fearsome predators. Young crocodiles begin by eating insects and other small prey, but adults eat fish and mammals up to the size of a Cape buffalo, which can weigh 1,500 pounds (680 kilograms). Crocodiles often lurk in waterholes, hidden below the water surface. When animals come to drink, the crocs power themselves out of the water using their tails and grab their victim. Often they drag their prey into the water and hold the animal underwater until it drowns.

Lizards

Most lizards are small animals, between 2.5 and 8 inches (6 and 20 centimeters) in length. For lizards this size the main prey are insects. The majority of lizards hunt by day, but geckos are a successful group because they have adapted to hunting at night. A few larger lizard species, such as snake lizards and monitor lizards, eat bigger prey. The largest monitor lizard, the Komodo dragon, often eats deer, pigs, and goats.

Crocodiles can spin themselves in the water with tremendous force. They do this when they have caught a large prey animal, to force its head underwater. They also do it to tear large pieces off their prey.

DIFFERENT JAWS

Turtles do not have teeth. Instead, they have a horny beak. In sea turtles, this beak is adapted to their diet. Green and black turtles have saw-tooth beaks, which are good for cutting up the sea grasses they eat. Loggerhead and ridley turtles have heavy, strong beaks for crushing and grinding the crabs and shellfish they feed on. Leatherback turtles eat only soft-bodied jellyfish, so their beak is delicate. Hawksbill turtles have a narrow beak for prying shrimps and other food out of cracks.

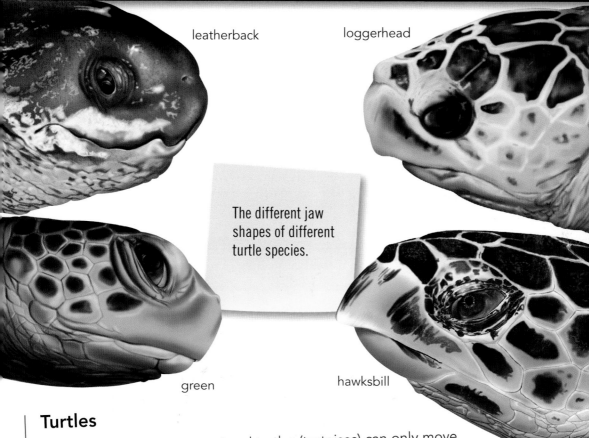

leatherback

loggerhead

The different jaw shapes of different turtle species.

green

hawksbill

Turtles

Most turtles are **omnivores**. Land turtles (tortoises) can only move slowly because of their heavy shells. They, therefore, feed mainly on insects or slow-moving prey such as slugs and snails.

In the water, many turtles, such as softshell or snapping turtles, are sit-and-wait hunters that eat frogs, worms, fish, and whatever else they can catch. Sea turtles are more active in the water. They can swim as fast as a person can run. Some sea turtles feed on the seabed, but leatherbacks travel long distances hunting for jellyfish.

17

Unusual Feeders

In any habitat, the competition for food and space is fierce. Some animals avoid the competition by finding unusual food sources. Other animals find unusual ways to catch their food that give them an edge over the competition.

Unpopular food

Few animals eat ants and termites. Ants and termites are social insects, and they attack enemies in large groups. However, thread snakes have adapted to actually live in ant or termite nests. Most animals would be attacked if they tried to get into an ant's nest, but thread snakes produce a special scent that calms down the soldier ants guarding the nest. This allows them to live in the nest and snack on the insects whenever they get hungry.

A nasty bite

Komodo dragons are predators, but also **scavengers**. The dead body of a goat or other animal will attract a whole group of these lizards.

When a Komodo dragon is hunting large animals, it usually hides by a well-used animal trail, then bursts out, ambushing its victim. The dragon only needs to get in one bite because its mouth is full of harmful bacteria that will quickly infect the wound. With its excellent sense of smell, the Komodo dragon then trails its victim until the injured animal dies. The dragon then devours the body.

A chameleon's tongue is long and has a sticky tip. It can extend its tongue to almost twice the length of its body. The tongue can shoot out to catch an insect in less than a hundredth of a second.

Marine iguanas can dive to depths of around 49 feet (15 meters). They normally dive for only a few minutes, but can survive at least half an hour underwater.

Sea vegetarians

Most iguanas are land animals, and several species live in deserts. However, marine iguanas on the Galapagos Islands have evolved the ability to swim and dive. They have webbed feet and their tails are flattened like those of sea snakes and crocodiles to help with swimming. All these adaptations allow marine iguanas to feed on a very unusual food source for lizards— the seaweed and other **algae** that grow on the seabed. They are the only lizards to feed in the ocean.

The seaweed that marine iguanas feed on is not a very popular food because it is full of salt. Most animals need salt in their food, but too much salt is dangerous. Marine iguanas have a special **gland** in their nose that gets rid of excess salt.

A TASTE FOR HUMANS

Crocodiles are not fussy eaters. They will attack any animal that comes within their range and is not too big to tackle. As a result, very large crocodiles sometimes kill and eat people. Nile crocodiles and saltwater crocodiles are the most dangerous species. Nile crocodiles are found in most rivers in Africa, while saltwater crocodiles live along the coasts of India and northern Australia.

19

Snake Camouflage

Many animals have **camouflage** to blend in with their environment. Camouflage works in two ways. It is an important adaptation that helps an animal avoid predators. Camouflage can hide a snake from enemies such as raccoons and hawks. Camouflage also is important for helping a snake get close to its prey without being seen.

The patterns on a gaboon viper are very striking against a plain background. But this photo shows how these strong patterns blend in on the forest floor.

Blending or blotchy

Most snakes are colored to blend in with their background. Desert snakes are sandy colored, while many tree snakes are green or brown. The eastern brown snake from eastern Australia can be brown, red, orange, or even black, depending on the habitat it lives in.

Many other snakes have patterns of blotches, diamonds, or stripes along their bodies. These patterns are known as **disruptive camouflage**. The different colored shapes break up the outline of the snake and make it very difficult to see. The gaboon viper is a large snake with bold brown, cream, and black patterns all over its body. These patterns stand out against a plain background. However, when a gaboon viper is lying coiled among the **leaf litter** in the central African rainforest, it is almost invisible. Gaboon vipers are ambush predators—they lie hidden in the leaf litter and wait for prey animals to pass by.

DANGEROUS COLORS

Some snakes, such as coral snakes, have bands of bright colors along their bodies. They stand out against their background rather than blend in. This bright coloring is a warning to predators—coral snakes have **venom** that is deadly even to humans. Animals that try to eat these snakes soon learn that the bright colors are a warning that says, "Keep away, I am poisonous!" The bright colors, therefore, protect the coral snake from possible predators.

Other, non-poisonous, snakes also take advantage of this adaptation. The North American milk snake has almost identical coloring to the poisonous coral snake. This makes predators think that the milk snake is also poisonous. So predators avoid this harmless mimic.

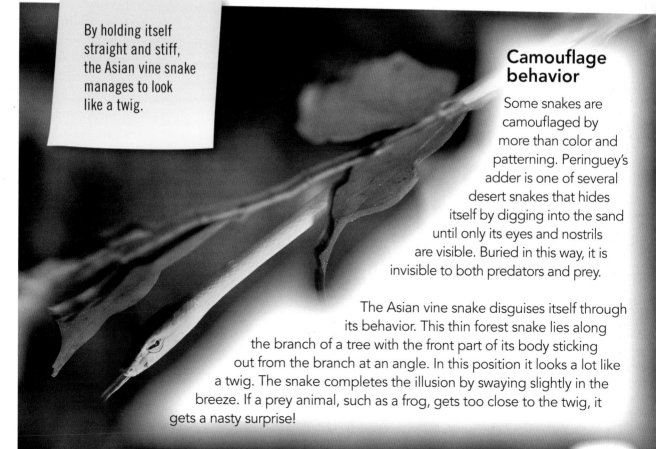

By holding itself straight and stiff, the Asian vine snake manages to look like a twig.

Camouflage behavior

Some snakes are camouflaged by more than color and patterning. Peringuey's adder is one of several desert snakes that hides itself by digging into the sand until only its eyes and nostrils are visible. Buried in this way, it is invisible to both predators and prey.

The Asian vine snake disguises itself through its behavior. This thin forest snake lies along the branch of a tree with the front part of its body sticking out from the branch at an angle. In this position it looks a lot like a twig. The snake completes the illusion by swaying slightly in the breeze. If a prey animal, such as a frog, gets too close to the twig, it gets a nasty surprise!

Camouflage in Other Reptiles

Most lizards are small animals. They have lots of enemies. Camouflage is an important part of their defense against predators. Turtles also use camouflage, both to hide from predators and to ambush their prey.

Can you see the lizard camouflaged on this rock?

Turtle shells

The colors and patterns of turtle shells are usually dull. This helps them blend in with their environment. Hawksbill turtles and other sea turtles have a darker top to their shell and a light underside. This kind of coloring makes them difficult to spot from above or below. Seen from above, the dark upper shell blends in with the dark background of the ocean depths or the seabed. From below, the light underside blends in with the background of light from the sea's surface. This is called **countershading**.

CROCODILES CAMOUFLAGE

Crocodiles and alligators use the water surface as part of their camouflage. With just their eyes and nostrils above water, the rest of their body is just a blurry shape when seen from the river bank. They often look like pieces of floating logs. Like sea turtles, crocodilians have light-colored bellies and dark backs, which make them harder to spot in the water.

Lizard camouflage

Most lizards are colored to blend in with their environment. Like snakes, many lizards are also speckled or patterned in a way that disrupts their shape and makes them harder to see. Horned lizards, crocodile lizards, and some other species have spines or plates in their skin that make them look like pieces of rock when they are still.

Lizards are generally very active animals. Camouflage colors and patterns are much less effective when an animal is moving. If a lizard feels threatened and has no hiding place nearby, it will freeze and rely on its camouflage to hide it. Lizards can stay still for long periods of time.

Changing colors

Chameleons are especially good at blending in with their surroundings, as they can change color to fit in with their environment. Combined with their leaf-like shape, this color-changing ability makes chameleons extremely difficult to spot when they are hunting. A few other lizards, such as the Malagasy flat-tailed gecko, can also change their color.

Chameleons sometimes change color because of their mood. The oranges and reds in this chameleon's coloring show that it is excited or annoyed.

Lizards can change their color because of special groups of cells in their skin. Each cell in the group contains a different **pigment**. By squeezing its muscles, the lizard can get the cells to change shape. In one shape the color of the cell is visible, but in another shape the cell's color does not show. By changing the shapes of the different cells, lizards can change to a variety of different colors.

Leaf Tails and Head Tails

A few reptile species have camouflage adaptations that go beyond colors and patterns. The reptile's whole body is adapted in some way to look like part of the environment.

Leaf-tailed geckos have the ability to make themselves lighter or darker, depending on the color of their background.

Leaf-like lizards

Many geckos have very good camouflage. Geckos need to find a safe way to rest during the day because they are active at night. One way to do this is to blend in perfectly with their environment.

The body and tail of a leaf-tailed gecko is flattened and shaped to look like a dead leaf. Veins in the skin mimic leaf veins, and the whole tail is twisted to make it look like a curled-up leaf. When it lies on a tree branch, fringes around the chin of the leaf-tailed gecko break up the outline of its head. Another mimic, the Sri Lankan kangaroo lizard, has legs that look like sticks and a body that looks like a dried leaf.

Other lizard adaptations

The young of the bushveldt lizard protect themselves through mimicry rather than camouflage. Their color and patterning look like those of the Anthia beetle, which squirts out an acidic spray when attacked. The young lizards also walk in a stiff way, to make their movements resemble that of a beetle.

Turtles in ambush

Another group of animals that rely on camouflage are ambush predators. An ambush predator is one that waits in hiding for its prey. The matamata, a kind of turtle, is an ambush predator that lives in lakes and slow-moving water in the Amazon River basin. It takes camouflage to an extreme. The lumps and bumps on the matamata's shell look a lot like stones. Its flattened, triangular head is covered with tufts and flaps of flesh, which make it look as if it is covered in weeds. Its superb camouflage can fool even the most wary of fish. When a prey animal comes close enough, the matamata suddenly opens its mouth and sucks in the unlucky victim.

Some of the skin flaps on the matamata turtle's head can sense movement in the water caused by prey close by.

GRAB MY TAIL!

Skinks are a large group of more than 1,300 lizard species. Most skinks are colored dull grays and browns to blend in with their habitat, but some species have evolved brightly colored tails. Like many other lizards, skinks have the ability to shed their tail if an enemy grabs it. Having a brightly colored tail is an adaptation that draws attention to the tail, distracting any predator from attacking the head and body.

Snake Defenses

The weapons that a snake uses when attacking prey can also be used to defend against enemies. However, many snakes have other defenses that they use when threatened. Whenever possible, a snake will run away or hide from its enemies. Snakes are experts at hiding because they can curl into a tight coil or spread themselves into a long line, which makes it difficult for a predator to know what to look for.

A cobra's head is small, but the hood makes it look much more threatening.

Looking bigger

If they are cornered, many snakes rear up and hiss or growl. Cobras have a flap of skin on either side of their head, which they can open up into a hood. The hood makes the cobra's head and neck look bigger. Hognose snakes also have a cobra-like hood. When threatened these harmless snakes spread their hood, hiss, and strike towards their attacker. South African boomslang snakes inflate their neck area when threatened.

The cottonmouth snake uses another kind of display to startle an attacker. It tips back its head and opens its mouth very wide to show its white lining. Cottonmouths and hognose snakes also produce an unpleasant smell when they are attacked, which puts the predator off.

BALL PYTHONS

Royal pythons are also known as ball pythons. This is because they curl up into a tight ball when they are threatened, with the head hidden in the center of the ball. This makes it difficult for a predator to attack the python.

Warning rattle

Other snakes make warning noises when under threat. The best known warning sound is the loud, buzzing rattle of a rattlesnake. There are 30 different species of rattlesnake most of which live only in North America. The rattle is produced by specialized dry scales in the tail. Scientists think that the rattle is an adaptation evolved to warn large grazing animals such as bison that the rattlesnake is there. A snake with a rattle is less likely to be stepped on than one without, so it gives rattlesnakes a survival advantage. One group of rattlesnakes lives on an island where there are no large grazing animals. These snakes have lost their rattle, as it no longer provides an advantage for survival.

Head in the sand

Many snakes do the opposite of cobras when an enemy threatens. They hide their head in the sand or soil and wave their tail. This defense has evolved to encourage predators to strike at the tail rather than the head. In pipe snakes the tail is flattened. When the pipe snake lifts its tail and waves it about it looks like a cobra's head.

This grass snake is playing dead. Grass snakes can stay motionless in this position for fifteen minutes or more.

Playing dead

Some smaller snakes, such as European grass snakes, play dead when attacked by a predator. They lie still, with their mouth open and tongue hanging out. Snakes that do this sometimes also produce a foul-smelling liquid, which perhaps suggests to predators that they are rotting and unpleasant to eat.

Other Reptile Defenses

Like snakes, other groups of reptiles also have defenses against predators. Some of these defenses are similar to those of snakes, but some are adaptations that snakes do not use.

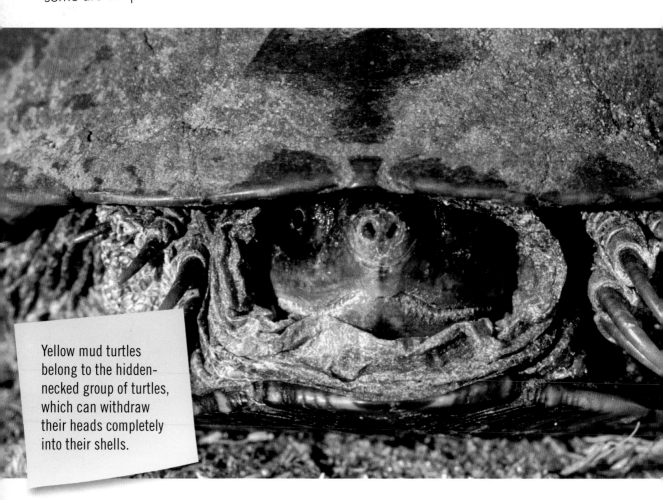

Yellow mud turtles belong to the hidden-necked group of turtles, which can withdraw their heads completely into their shells.

Armored home

Armor is one form of defense that has arisen in other reptile groups, but not among snakes. Turtles have survived for over 200 million years, and an important part of their success is their tough shell, which provides portable protection from predators. When attacked, a turtle draws its head and legs into its shell and sits tight. In their armored casing, turtles are safe from all but a few predators.

Turtles can be divided into two groups, depending on how they draw in their heads. Hidden-necked turtles can draw in their heads completely, while side-necked turtles simply fold their head sideways under the front edge of the shell.

More armor

Many crocodilians and lizards are also armored. Thorny devils and armadillo lizards are armored with large spikes that make them hard to eat. When an armadillo lizard is threatened, it puts its tail in its mouth. This protects the lizards soft belly area, and leaves the predator with a very thorny mouthful.

All crocodilians have plates of bony armor just under the skin all along their back. In some species, such as saltwater crocodiles, the bony plates are thin and there is no armor plating on the neck and shoulders. Other crocodilians, such as the black caiman, have thick, tough armor along the back and neck.

EXTRA STRONG SHELL

The ornate box turtle lives on the grasslands of North America. It feeds on insects in cow dung, so it often looks for food close to cattle. To avoid being trampled on, the box turtle has a high, domed shell. The domed shape makes the shell extra strong. Also, a cow's foot is more likely to slip off a high dome than a flattened shell.

Shedding the tail

Another important defense mechanism in lizards is tail-shedding. If a predator grabs their tail, most lizards can shed part of the tail and escape. They can do this because some of the bones in the tail are weak and break easily. The muscles and blood vessels also are adapted to allow all or part of the tail to be shed quickly.

This green lizard has shed its tail to escape from danger. Although the tail will grow back, it will never be as long, and the new tail cannot be shed.

Spitting, Bleeding, and Scare Tactics

The relationship between a predator and its prey is always changing. Each time a predator evolves new weapons or ways of attacking its prey, the prey animals develop new defenses. Some reptiles have developed some amazing defenses in response to the threat of predators.

Dangerous spit

If a spitting cobra is threatened, it rears up, spreads its hood, and spits venom in the eyes of its enemy. It can hit a predator from nearly ten feet (more than three meters) away. The venom causes temporary blindness and great pain. If a human gets cobra venom in his or her eye, it causes great irritation and, if left untreated, can cause permanent blindness.

Horned lizards from North America do not spit **venom**, but they can shoot liquid at their attackers. If a horned lizard is grabbed by a predator, it squirts blood from special sinuses (blood-filled spaces around its eyes). The blood is foul tasting and often makes the predator let go.

Spitting cobras spit by blowing hard at the same time as letting venom drip from their fangs.

Fighting predators

Like snakes, some lizards play dead or become very rigid if attacked. This may not seem like much of a defense, but many predators have an attack reflex that makes them grab prey that moves quickly. If the prey stays still, they are less interested.

Other lizards defend themselves by trying to startle their enemies. Again, this may not seem like a very effective defense, but if a lizard can make an attacker pause for just a few seconds, it may give the lizard enough time to scurry away to safety.

Frilled lizards startle their enemies by opening their mouth wide and spreading a large flap of skin around the neck. This makes the lizard suddenly look much larger and possibly dangerous, which often makes the predator pause. Blue-tongued skinks from Australia have a very unusual defense against enemies. They puff up their bodies, hiss, and stick out their bright blue tongues. As with the frilled lizard, the shock can give the skink just enough time to escape.

The Australian frilled lizard is usually small and harmless looking. However, when it makes its threat display, it looks fearsome.

INVISIBLE ENEMIES

One kind of defense in crocodiles and alligators is against invisible enemies—bacteria and other microscopic germs. The water that crocodilians live in is often dirty and full of disease-causing bacteria. Yet the wounds they get in fights and when catching their prey rarely get infected. Scientists have discovered that crocodilians' blood contains a chemical that kills bacteria. This chemical is different from the drugs doctors normally use to fight infections. Scientists may be able to develop a whole new range of useful drugs for humans based on these chemicals.

Snake Reproduction

Snakes usually hunt alone and rarely gather in groups with other snakes. However, some species do get together at certain times of year. Male and female snakes also meet up to mate.

Male garter snakes swarm over each other in a frenzy—each one trying to mate with a single female.

Snake meetings

Rattlesnakes and garter snakes often hibernate together. When they emerge from hibernation in spring, garter snakes usually mate immediately. Where large numbers of garter snakes are gathered in one place, many males compete to mate with one female. They form a twisting ball of snakes, with the female at the center.

Not all snakes hibernate together. Snakes that live alone need a way to find a mate. In most snakes, females that are ready to mate produce a special scent, which they leave behind them wherever they go. Any male that comes across the scent follows the trail to find the female.

Garter snakes are not the only species in which the males compete for females. Mambas, vipers, and rattlesnakes also do this. Two males that want to mate with the same female wrestle with each other. The snakes rear up and twine around each other, each one trying to force the other to the ground. The strongest male wins and gets to mate with the female. This means that only the strongest males get to mate.

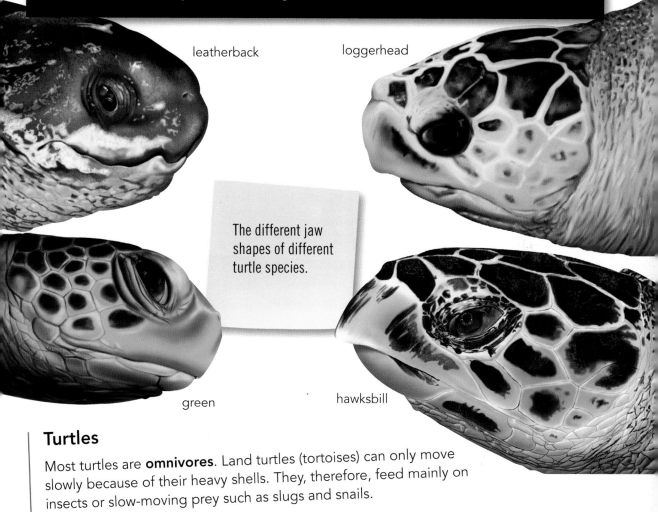